SCHIRMER'S LIBRARY
OF MUSICAL CLASSICS

Vol. 2034

Dmitri Kabalevsky

The Sonatinas

For Piano

ISBN 978-0-7935-8927-2

G. SCHIRMER, Inc.

DISTRIBUTED BY

HAL•LEONARD®
CORPORATION

7777 W. BLUEMOUND RD. P.O. BOX 13819 MILWAUKEE, WI 53213

SONATINA No. 1

Dmitri Kabalevsky, Op. 13, No. 1
Edited by Luise Vosgerchian

I

Allegro assai e lusingando

II

III

SONATINA No. 2

I

Dmitri Kabalevsky, Op. 13, No. 2

Allegro non troppo Risoluto

II

Sostenuto

III

Vivace